ENOUGH OF

ANNE STEVENSON

Enough of Green

774565
821

OXFORD LONDON NEW YORK
OXFORD UNIVERSITY PRESS
1977

Oxford University Press, Walton Street, Oxford OX2 6DP

OXFORD LONDON GLASGOW NEW YORK
TORONTO MELBOURNE WELLINGTON CAPE TOWN
IBADAN NAIROBI DAR ES SALAAM LUSAKA
KUALA LUMPUR SINGAPORE JAKARTA HONG KONG TOKYO
DELHI BOMBAY CALCUTTA MADRAS KARACHI

British Library Cataloguing in Publication Data

Stevenson, Anne
   Enough of green.
   I. Title
   821'.9'14   PR6069.T45   77-30081
   ISBN 0-19-211874-9

*Printed in Great Britain by
The Bowering Press Ltd
Plymouth*

To Be a Poet

You must always be alone.
But don't beg a soupscrap of charity
or birdcrumb of tolerance.
Shift for yourself.
As furniture heaves off your life
you'll love your deliverance.

Until loneliness slips in, scrawny
and hungry, Miss Loneliness, over the
barrenness, bribing with company.
Restlessness, one of her attendants.
And the drunk twins, of course,
Memory and Remorse.

Refuse them. Stay faithful to Silence, just
Silence, sliding between that breath
and now this breath, severing the tick
from the tock on the alarm clock,
measuring the absence of else.
And the presence, the privilege.

Acknowledgements

Some of the poems in this collection have been published by *The Listener*, *The Times Literary Supplement*, *The New Review*, *Lines Review*, *The Scotsman*, *Encounter*, *Stand*, *Outposts*, *Oxford Poetry Now*, *Seagate* (Dundee) and *Murid*. 'A Summer Place' was included in *New Poems 1976–77* (ed. Howard Sergeant, Hutchinson), 'North Sea off Carnoustie' and 'Fire and the Tide' were included in *Scottish Poetry 8* (Carcanet, 1975), and 'With my Sons at Boarhills' in *Scottish Poetry 9* (Carcanet, 1976). 'Aberdeen', 'Night Wind, Dundee', 'By the Boat House, Oxford' and 'Mallaig Harbour Resembles Heaven in Spring Sunlight' were published in the Arts Council's *New Poetry 1*' 1975.

I am grateful to my friends and colleagues in Dundee and to many friends in Oxford for advice and encouragement. I wish particularly to thank Andrew Motion for suggesting the title.

All those of the 'Seagate' circle in Dundee contributed more to this volume than they know. I am also grateful to Mrs E. M. Chilver and my fellow fellows of Lady Margaret Hall for their sympathetic good will, and as always to my husband, Mark Elvin.

Contents

Those that he'll have,
to G.F.D.

The Sun Appears in November

When trees are bare,
when ground is more glowing than summer,
in sun, in November,
you can see what lay under
confusing eloquence of green.

Bare boughs in their cunning
twist this way and that way
trying to persuade by crooked reasoning.
But trees are constrained from within
to conform to skeleton.

Nothing they put on
will equal these lines of cold branches,
the willows in bunches,
birches like lightning,
transparent in brown spinneys, beeches.

North Sea off Carnoustie

For Jean Rubens

You know it by the northern look of the shore,
by the salt-worried faces,
by an absence of trees, an abundance of lighthouses.
It's a serious ocean.

Along marram-scarred, sandbitten margins
wired roofs straggle out to where
a cold little holiday fair
has floated in and pitched itself
safely near the prairie of the golf course.
Coloured lights are sunk deep into the solid wind,
but all they've caught is a pair of lovers
and three silly boys.
Everyone else has a dog.
Or a room to get to.

The smells are of fish and of sewage and cut grass.
Oystercatchers, doubtful of habitation,
clamour 'weep, weep, weep' as they fuss over
scummy black rocks the tide leaves for them.

The sea is as near as we come to another world.

But there in your stony and windswept garden
a blackbird is confirming the grip of the land.
'You, you,' he murmurs, dark purple in his voice.

And now in far quarters of the horizon
lighthouses are awake, sending messages—
invitations to the landlocked,
warnings to the experienced,
but to anyone returning from the planet ocean,
candles in the windows of a safe earth.

Fire and the Tide

Fire struggles in the chimney like an animal.
It's caught in a life,
as when the tide pulls the Tay out
scarring predictable mudscape—
seawater's knifework
notching quick runnel and channel.

That's how you remember
the alternative lives.
You saw them, could never have lived them.
A ribbon of birds is pulled raggedly over November.
You're pulled between now and the way you will not escape.

The Mudtower

And again, without snow, a new year.
As for fifty years, a thousand years, the air
returns the child-blue rage of the river.
Six swans rise aloud from the estuary,
ferrying tremendous souls to the pond by the playground.
They're coming for me! No. I'm a part of the scenery.
They fly low, taking no interest in migratory ladies.

The stone town stumbles downhill to untidy mudflats—
high square houses, shivering in windows, the street of shops,
the church and clocktower, school, the four worn pubs
artfully spaced between dry rows of white cottages.
Then council flats, fire station, rusty gasometer,
timber yard baying out its clean smell of pinewood.
Then grass, swings, mud. The wilted estuary.

You could say that the winter's asleep in the harbour's arm.
Two sloops with their heads on their backs are sleeping there
                                        peacefully.

Far out in the tide's slum, in the arm of the sand-spit,
the mudtower wades in the giving and taking water.

Its uses—if it ever had uses—have been abandoned.
The low door's a mouth. Slit eyes stab the pinnacle.
Its lovethrust is up from the mud it seems to be made of.
Surely it's alive and hibernating, Pictish and animal.
The sea birds can hear it breathing in its skin or shrine.

How those lighthouses, airing their bones on the coast,
hate the mudtower! They hold their white messages aloft
like saints bearing scriptures.

As the water withdraws, the mudtower steps out on the land.
Watch the fierce, driven, hot-looking
scuttlings of redshanks, the beaks of the oystercatchers.
Struggle and panic. Struggle and panic.
Mud's rituals resume. The priest-gulls flap to the kill.
Now high flocks of sandpipers, wings made of sunlight,
flicker as snow flickers, blown from those inland hills.

With my Sons at Boarhills

Gulls think it is for them
that the wormy sand rises,
brooding on its few rights,
losing its war with water.

The mussel flats ooze out,
and now the barnacled, embossed
stacked rocks are pedestals for strangers,
for my own strange sons,
scraping in the pool,
imperilling their pure reflections.

Their bodies are less beautiful than
blue heaven's pleiades of herring gulls,
or gannets, or that sloop's sail
sawtoothing the sea as if its
scenery were out of date, as if its
photographs had all been taken:
two boys left naked in a sloughed off summer,
skins and articulate backbones,
fossils for scrapbook or cluttered mantelpiece.

If you look now, quickly and askance,
you can see how the camera's eye
perfected what was motion and chance before
it clicked on this day and childhood snapshot,
scarcely seen beside
hunched rugby stripes and ugly uniforms—
shy, familiar grins in a waste of faces.

My knee joints ache and crack
as I kneel to my room's fire, feeding it.
Steam wreathes from my teacup, clouding
the graduate, the lieutenant, the weddings,
the significant man of letters, the politician
smiling from his short victory . . .

Faces I washed and scolded, only
watched as my each child laboured from his own womb,
bringing forth, without me, men who must
call me mother, love or reassess me
as their barest needs dictate, return
dreaming, rarely to this saltpool in memory,
naked on a morning full of see-through jellyfish,
with the tide out and the gulls out
grazing on healed beaches,
while sea-thrift blazes by the dry path,
and the sail stops cutting the water to pieces
and heads for some named port inland.

Their voices return like footprints over the sandflats,
permanent, impermanent, salt and sensuous
as the sea is, in its frame, its myth.

B

The Exhibition
For Alasdair Gray

The exhibition is of
  all the exhibited people
    gathered together at the exhibition.

How pleasing. Everyone is at ease.
  The canvasses are amiably walking around
    choosing faces which are

cut out of smooth brown packing paper,
  pasted meticulously in the spaces
    wearing their names.

How can they fail to be flattered,
  these figures who, in frames,
    stay distressingly apart from one another,

but when meeting themselves on the walls
  are so delighted?
    That woman lying naked on the bed,

for instance, stops
  brooding over her weakness of will
    and admires her thighs.

And the man without shoes, in his necktie,
  approves his cool sense of detachment,
    his power to despatch it and rise.

Yes, it's all satisfactory self-fulfilment—
  admirer and admired so embraced
    there's no place for the past,

though behind both paint and gallery
   you can see that some old city is
      thinning to dissolution.

Distances between shoulder and shoulder
   and eye and eye grow wider as the
      waste lots fill up with workers'

rubble: brokenhearts, hangovers, torn sheets,
   yards of mattress stuffing, bottles,
      cigarette butts, used newspapers.

Enlightened, momentarily spared,
   the invited say 'thank you' and
      go in their separate directions.

Now the pictures, left holding their
   bodies and heads, have no chance of
      changing things at all by making connections.

East Coast

Summer

Ebb day, full tide.
Yellowhammers whistling in fullblown bushes.
Scent of wet cypresses, lavender, roses.
Dying storm, veiled like a bride.

The Bench

Steep path to where the wheatfields' yellow
makes a plush gilt frame for the town.
A bench there—no back but a view—
for lovers, dog-walkers, poets. Tired men
with sensational newspapers climb there too.

Boating Pool at Night

Enormous, this fragment of July
stretched between pool and shallow night,
house   house
light   light
sky   in the whole sky.

Winter Flowers

For Kiff and Adele Rathbone

I don't know why at all,
but when, that winter evening,
you came with fists full of blazing summer flowers,
a brick fell out of the wall
enclosing Eden, leaving
a peephole, just for a moment ours,
through which we saw the simultaneous seasons,
dying, breeding, bearing, fixed like stars;
and the trees—one hoary, dangerous with wisdom,
one green with the impossibility of years.

The Lighthouse

Though I did not intend
on my journey that it should end
at this lighthouse and town
surrounded by tidewater's flat brown
halo of muddy sand
(opening and closing like a hand)
clearly on looking back I see
the road led here inevitably.

With its litter of feathers and shells it bends
on further, blends
with blue water further than I can see.
And is what will be.
The bay—so beautiful.
I—only its animal.
And the lighthouse, ever unsatisfied,
glutted in the tide.

Night Wind, Dundee

At sundown, a seaforce that gulls rode or fell through.
The small snow is surf. Eddies of strong air
swarm up old tenements. Listen! My window's
late rat-tat-tat guns back at who and whose enemy
milked the sky's agates, polished its ebony.
Warm rooms are lit up in bare blocks of concrete.
Someone's ripped cobwebs from a great vault's rafters,
revealing a moonface, a starfield,
barbarian Orion crucified in God's heaven.

Aberdeen

Old daughter with a rich future,
that's blueveined Aberdeen,
reeking of fish, breathing sea air
like atomized pewter. Her clean
gothic ribs rattle protests to the
spiky gusts. Poor girl.
She's got to marry oil.
Nobody who loves her wants to save her.

Mallaig Harbour Resembles Heaven in Spring Sunlight

Reach Mallaig and discover
Heaven is real.
Herring stir the harbour
into haloes of seagulls, or else
birds in free, dissonant chorus
are themselves white angels.

The ships glide in gracefully,
souls assured of their salvation,
not pretty
but exclusive and competent.

A work-a-day place. We should have known it.
How could we have imagined it other
than as home for the unimpeded,
the locality of accomplishment?

Ragwort

They won't let railways alone, those yellow flowers.
They're that remorseless joy of dereliction
darkest banks exhale like vivid breath
as bricks divide to let them root between.
How every falling place concocts their smile,
taking what's left and making a song of it.

By the Boat House, Oxford

They belong here in their own quenched country.
I had forgotten nice women could be so nice,
smiling beside large sons on the makeshift quay,
frail, behind pale faces and hurt eyes.

Their husbands are plainly superior, with them, without them.
Their boys wear privilege like a clear inheritance, easily.
(Now a swan's neck couples with its own reflection,
making in the simple water a perfect 3.)

The punts seem resigned to an unexciting mooring.
But the women? It's hard to tell. Do their fine grey hairs
and filament lips approve or disdain the loving
that living alone, or else lonely in pairs, impairs?

Ruin

Well, they're gone, long gone,
and the land they called theirs
owns them now, without knowing
anyone cares.

What they lived to be doing
has been done, long done.
It's as if looking back
were to look further on.

For their money and saws
and their queer human knack
they gained these few acres,
achieved this wreck.

Beneath choke-cherry, broadfern
bramble and mullein,
boulders they'll build from,
bedrooms they'll lie in.

A Summer Place

You know that house she called home,
so sleek, so clapboard-white,
that used to be some country jobber's blight
or scab on our hill's arm.
You can see the two cellars of the barn,
stones still squatting where the fellow stacked them.

He worked the place as a farm,
though how, with stones for soil, she never knew.
Partly she hoped he'd been a poet, too—
why else hang Haystack mountain and its view
from north-west windows?
It was the view she bought it for. He'd gone.
The house sagged on its frame. The barns were down.

The use she saw for it was not to be
of use. A summer place. A lovely
setting where fine minds could graze
at leisure on long summer days
and gather books from bushes, phrase by phrase.
Work would be thought. A tractor bought for play
would scare unnecessary ugly scrub away.

A white gem set on a green silk glove
she bought and owned there.
And summers wore it, just as she would wear
each summer like a dress of sacred air
until the house was half compounded of
foundations, beams and paint, half of her love.

She lived profoundly, felt, wrote from her heart,
knew each confessional songbird by its voice,
cloistered her garden with bee balm and fanning iris,
sat, stained by sunsets, in a vault of noise

listening through cricket prayer for whitethroat,
hermit thrush—and couldn't keep it out,
the shade of something wrong, a fear, a doubt,

as though she heard the house stir in its plaster,
stones depart unsteadily from walls,
the woods, unwatched, stretch out their roots like claws
and tear through careful fences, fiercer than saws.
Something alive lived under her mind-cropped pasture,
hated the house—or worse, loved, hungering after
its perfectly closed compactness, breathed disaster.

She dreamed or daydreamed what it might have come to,
the house itself, wanting the view
to take it, and the view's love gathering into
brambles, tendrils, trunks of maples, needing
her every window, entering, seeding . . .
Fear of attack kept her from sleeping,
kept her awake in her white room, pacing, weeping.

But you see the place still stands there, pretty as new.
Whatever she thought the mountain and trees would do,
they did—and took her with them—and withdrew.

Thales and Li Po

Thales, out
scanning the stars for truth,
walked into a well.
Li Po fell in love
with the moon's
reflection
in the Yellow River.

Which was the best way to die?
It doesn't matter.
Try an analysis of sky, or
passionate, ignorant,
embrace a lie.

Path

Aged by rains
and cool under pulsing trees,
the summer path is paved with winter leaves.
Roots lace it like an old man's veins.

And nothing in field, on hill can so appal
burnt August and its transitory walker
as this which leads a summer
towards its fall.

Now under cover
of the leopard pelt
of that lean way, more heat, more passions felt
than ever in shimmering field by usual lover.

Fanged with surprising light, the path means harm.
Not calm, not comfort, not release from love.
White innocent motes of dust
rise up and swarm.

Good-bye! Good-bye!

The expected train
is about to abandon the station.
the plane ceases to depend
on the measured tarmac. Yes,
O yes, we will never require them again.
We can say good-bye to items we're by now
deadly bored with—
weather we tolerated and forgot,
streets that escorted us blindfold
through poisonous traffic. And look!
There's a lady in a pink chiffon headscarf,
waving, clutching her handbag—
now the thin balding gentleman waves,
and his granddaughter, kissing her hand
and waving from the tall son's shoulder.
The young mother waves last,
thinking of the hand-crocheted coat
and the glistening hair ribbon.

Good-bye! Good-bye! We will never see you again.

Black headlines whirl out on the slipstream,
the screams getting smaller.
Are those hundred of square narrow pinnacles
tenements or graves?
Perhaps they are instruments of war,
whatever wars are.
Press on. It doesn't matter.
Whatever the wars were about
they have to be over.
The years are raked into heaps around
plenty of monuments.
The dead are buried.
Survivors come peaceably together,
the men with the women, inevitably.

Will those lovers be able to tear themselves away from their kiss?

The schoolboy's embarrassed.
The spinster, who has lived on yoghurt
fifty years in an agony of worthiness,
burrows in a brown paper bag for spiritual support.
Out, travelling free, we must leave all this
turbulence behind us.
The team doesn't notice.
The drunk looks for sympathy for himself.
Don't be afraid of that salesman with the buffalo chin.
You're quite, quite alone
when you get this near the millennium.

Good-bye! Good-bye! Or as I was about to say,
Come in.

Temporarily in Oxford

Where they will bury me
I don't know
Many places might not be
sorry to store me.

The Midwest has right of origin.
Already it has welcomed my mother
to its flat sheets.

The English fens that bore me
have been close curiously often.
It seems I can't get away from
dampness and learning.

If I stay where I am
I could sleep in this educated dirt.

But if they are kind
they'll burn me and
send me to Vermont.

I'd be an education for the trees
and would relish, really,
flaring into maple each October—
my scarlet letter to you.

Your stormy north is possible.
You will be there, engrossed in its peat.

It would be handy not to have to
cross the whole Atlantic
each time I wanted to
lift up the turf
and slip in beside you.

c

Posted

Instead of your letter
a late train out of the north
plunges towards London, bringing me down
to myself.

Instead of your words
this scribble inside my skin
is literature your hand, my hand
sealed in.

It's all we could never
say but only do.
I dare not read for fear of
losing you,

but fold myself
unopened—though I wrote
as much of it as you—into
this note

which I'll receive,
once I come back to me,
tear open, study, scarcely believe
I see.

Hotel in the City

Together, alone, brief guests of the darkness
we listen to the year being torn down around us.
At a shake of wet flanks, today like an avalanche—
tomorrow in dirty fur prowling the streets,
growl of a century that won't lie down.
Now its dazzle slips under the fringe of the curtain,
dragging the city in over the sheets.

Hide in my hand. Lend me your skin.
Be blind and be deaf and escape by touch
the light that pursues us and knows our names,
the sound of those trains going different directions.

Wanted

'I want you forever and ever' I want to say.
Meaning that no night passes, and no day
without your being wished for, thought of,
abstract as age to youth, or war in peace.
Will the ache of your always absence ever cease?
Or will we be someday, somewhere, together enough
for you to keep turning pages till night is grey?
For me to want you away?

Drought

After the exhilaration of the peaks
look on, look back—
infatuations—screes parched to their rock—
a river of dry water scours dry land—
those twisted, black, alluvial obsessions—
memory is a river without rain.

Restore the flood of simple speech again,
the affectionate plash of word thrown over pain,
the brown of perpetual flowing where your hand
thrusts white beneath the cold of sliding waters,
invites, invents, forgives its own distortion,
gripping the green of live and rooted matters.

After the End of It

You gave and gave,
and now you say you're poor.
I'm in your debt, you say,
and there's no way to repay you
but by my giving more.

Your pound of flesh is what you must have?
Here's what I've saved.

This sip of wine is yours,
this sieve of laughter. Yours,
too, these broken haloes
from my cigarette, these coals
that flicker when the salt wind howls
and the letter box blinks like a loud
eyelid over the empty floor.

I'll send this, too, this gale between rains,
this wild day. Its cold is so cold
I want to break it into panes
like new ice on a pond; then pay it
pain by pain to your account.
Let it freeze us both into some numb country!
Giving and taking might be the same there.
A future of measurement and blame
gone in a few bitter minutes.

Cain

Lord have mercy upon the angry.
The anguished can take care of each other.
The angels will take care of themselves.
But the angry have no daughters or mothers;
only brute brothers, themselves.
Hearing that faint 'Abel, Abel' they stop their ears.
Watching that approved flame snake to the sky
they beat stubby blades out of ploughshares,
cut the sun out of the air,
Stamp on small fires they might have seen by.

Resurrection

Surprised by spring,
by the green light fallen like snow
in a single evening,
by hawthorn, blackthorn, willow,
meadow—everything
woken again after how many thousand years?
As if there had been no years.

That generous throat
is a blackbird's. Now, a thrush.
And that ribbon flung out,
that silk voice, is a chaffinch's rush
to his grace-note.
Birds woo, or apportion the innocent air they're made for.
Whom do they sing for?

Old man by the river
spread out like a cross in the sun
feet bare
and stared at by three grubby children,
you've made it again, and yes we'll inherit a summer.
Always the same green clamouring fells you that wakes you.
And you have to start living again when it wakes you.

The Price

The fear of loneliness, the wish
to be alone;
love grown rank as seeding grass
in every room,
and anger at it, raging at it
storming it down.

Also that four-walled chrysalis
and impediment, home;
that lamp and hearth, that easy fit
of bed to bone;
those children, too, sharp witnesses
of all I've done.

My dear, the ropes that bind us
are safe to hold;
the walls that crush us keep us
from the cold.
I know the price and still I pay it, pay it—
words, their furtive kiss,
illicit gold.

In the Orchard

Black bird, black voice,
almost the shadow of a voice,
so kind to this tired summer sky,
a rim of night around it,
yet almost an echo of today,
all the days since that first
soft guttural disaster
gave us 'apple' and 'tree'
and all that transpired thereafter
in the city of the tongue.

Blackbird, so old, so young, so
lucky to be stricken with a song
you can never choose away from.

The Sirens are Virtuous

They are not what you think.
The sirens are virtuous.
Very smart. Very dedicated.
In their true form
ladies. Not women. Not fish.
They abhor boring islands.
But wherever a human vortex is,
there they are at the centre.

'Come unto me, all ye who labour
and are weary without reason
and I will give you
fresh causes of feverish concern,'
sings one, penetrating the plugged ears
of the never-at-rest.

Looking guiltily inward
from under the O, slowing swinging
of Ought, these men are terrified—
its noose lowering—
so they witness with relief
its transformation into a mouth.
Lips. Warmth. Breath.
What is it to them
that it is shouting,
not kissing?

The ladies are professionals,
they divide and devour
professionally.
Helmsman from the helm.
Herdsman from the herd.
Though always there is one
who will not peel off and die joyfully,

in a good season
thousands can be loved, sucked,
drained, disposed of.

'There, our laps are full,'
cry the ladies at intervals,
shaking out their skirts,
shaking the bones from their aprons.
'And how we adored them, the drab cockatoos,
the serious darlings, the nearly salvational
whey-faced fellows of feverish concern.'

The Race

The small are winning.
They don't know they are winning.
They think they are behind.
They can't see through the tall
who look as though they're winning
from behind.

The small are all behind.
They think there is a place to end.
They think there is a place to win.
But they can't see who is winning.
We're winning, the tall pretend,
the tall who are just beginning
to realize the end
is the beginning.

Now the tall are thinning.
The small are not far back.
It seems the track won't end.
Its straightness is a bend.
In fact, the track
is winning
as the tall who were winning
fall behind
while the small who were behind
are tall and winning.

And now the small are winning
who are behind.

Minister

We're going to need the minister
to help this heavy body into the ground.

But he won't dig the hole.
Others who are stronger and weaker will have to do that.
And he won't wipe his nose and his eyes.
Others who are weaker and stronger will have to do that.
And he won't bake cakes or take care of the kids—
women's work—anyway,
what would they do at a time like this
if they didn't do that?

No, we'll get the minister to come
and take care of the words.

He doesn't have to make them up.
He doesn't have to say them well.
He doesn't have to like them
so long as they agree to obey him.

We have to have the minister
so the words will know where to go.

Imagine them circling and circling
the confusing cemetery.
Imagine them roving the earth
without anywhere to rest.

Doctor

I am the doctor.
It is my joy to make people well.
It's convenient, of course, if they sicken
in conventional ways. The mother like a caught moth
fluttering with bedpan by the bed.
The bigger kids fighting and teasing,
a husband in the cobwebs, a smell of stale dinner—
it has to be cooked and not eaten.

To this kind of fireside
I always bring hope and encouragement.
I approach through my smile and display
my incredible instruments. I refuse cups of tea
and wrapped barley sugar. Health? Yes,
yes, you can pick it alive from my lips.
'Little boy, little boy.'
His eyes open, gushing with confidence.
'Little boy, little boy.'
He gets well. He decides to grow up.

Historians

Historians who
sleep through history
sleepwalk in the snow,
wanting the final snow
to save their pages—
inky roofs of all they
knew or know.

Snow leaves no salvages.
No sound is heard.
Each individual flake
covers a word.

Swimmer

This man who re-enters the water so
desires Ordovician freedom that he gives up air.
The waves shut greenly. He is hugged by his first horizons.
Islands in his two-fold vision make and
unmake themselves. Forests that fish know,
but have never made maps of, glow
in the dangerous O of his eye and brain;
arrange that in his long look backward
he see no less than the whole way he has come,
no more than the world he keeps wrecking
and making in memory, where the ocean asks to be visited,
where rivers believe in the sea.

D

Graves with Children

In summer
our children swarm over us
into their weather,
the thresh of bare foot over foot
erases our names.
Our stories no longer have
violence enough to allure them,
they take no interest
in the heavy freight of our toys.
Careless, irreverent,
they rise out of your stone,
my stone,
disappear through chinks
of impassable light and noise.
Listen—
there's wind in the grass,
there's rain in the moss,
then silence, winter,
those unanswerable girls and boys.

Early Rain

Imagine a city rooted in its reflections.
Or imagine reflections
where there ought to be a city,
where there would be a city, certainly,
if there were people.
As yet there are no people, only doors
grieving over eighteenth-century pediments,
porticos drilling through a black lake.
Try to imagine the lights, too,
white and glittering,
a few more red than glittering,
bleeding outrageously under false names.

Imagine the foundations of such a city,
you and I, perhaps, asleep in a room,
but buried beneath the cornerstone all the same.

Meniscus

The moon at its two extremes,
promise and reminiscence,
future and past succeeding each other,
the rim of a continuous event.

These eyes which contain the moon
in the suspect lens of an existence,
guiding it from crescent to crescent
as from mirror to distorting mirror.

The good bones sheathed in my skin,
the remarkable knees and elbows
working without audible complaint
in the salty caves of their fitting.

My cup overfilled at the brim
and beyond the belief of the brim.
Absolved by the power of the lip
from the necessity of falling.

Respectable House

Worth keeping your foot in the door.
Worth letting the lamplight stripe your shoe
and escape in the dark behind you.

Worth the candle-width of a velvet floor,
the swell of a stair, a tinkle of glasses,
and overheard—rising and flaring—those fortunate voices.

Push open the door. More. And a little more.
You seem to be welcome. You can't help stepping inside.
You see how light and its residents have lied.

You see what the gun on the table has to be used for.

Colours

Enough of green
though to remember childhood
is to stand in uneasy radiance
under those trees.

Enough yellow.
We are looking back
over our shoulders, telling our children
to be happy.

Try to forget about red.
Leave it to the professionals.
But perceive heaven as a density
blue enough to abolish the stars.

As long as the rainbow lasts
the company stays.

Of black there is never enough.

One by one the lights in the house go out.
Step over the threshold. Forget
to take my hand.